Robert Stetson

MAKE YOUR PAPERBACK 4 FREE

It's FREE 4 YOU and you make $$$

Robert Stetson

ISBN-10:   1480242454
ISBN-13: 978-1480242456

MAKE YOUR PAPERBACK 4 FREE

MAKE YOUR PAPERBACK 4 FREE
Text copyright © 2012
Robert Stetson All Rights Reserved

Preface

I'm going to show you how to make that paperback, get it into hard copy circulation and collect your royalties, for FREE.

I have heard that maybe 10% of the population owns an E-Reader. I've also heard that 3% of the population reads books at all. That means your target market is about .3% (That's point 3 percent). My experience is that almost 100% of the population has hands and eyes and most of them can actually read.

You probably wrote your EBook because you had a desire to write. You worked hours slaving at the computer to get every drop of sweat down on that document.

I bet you even tried to find a publisher or an agent, didn't you. The literary world has beaten you to a pulp.

Then you uploaded it to become an EBook. When the excitement of having your book published wore off, you started tracking it. Come on, admit it… You logged on several times a day to see if anyone was buying it. What did you make this month on that book, maybe $ 24.00? Now you're saying, "I did all that for 13 cents an hour?

Time to fight back, Bunkie. Let's take that EBook and make it into something you can wrap your fist around. Make it a paperback and put hard copy on the bookstore shelves! Let me show you how to make some real money.

If your book is a hit and those snooty agents call, just tell them, "No thanks, I'm all set." They take a cut of your money and because you're new, the publisher might only give you 5%.

DISCLAIMER

I hate disclaimers, don't you? But hold on. This is important and I want to be completely honest with you up front.

If you don't know how to use Microsoft Word, then hire someone to do this for you. I'm not looking to drum up business here. I'm hoping you can do it. You can pay Amazon to do it for you.

I can tell you how to get this done, but I can't do it for you. If you can use Microsoft Word, then this should work for you just fine. I use Microsoft Word 2010. If you have an older version it may not be as easy to get things set up just right, but you should still be able to get it working without much more hassle.

MAKE YOUR PAPERBACK 4 FREE

Table of Contents

Chapter 1 Why Publish a Paperback?   1

Chapter 2 Amazon as a Self-Publisher   6

Chapter 3 How to Do It Step by Step   11

Chapter 4 Formatting your Book with MS Word 21

Chapter 5 Building Your Cover   36

Chapter 8 Paperback Marketing is Easy   47

Chapter 6 Price and Release Your Book   54

Chapter 7 Sit Back and Make the MONEY   58

Chapter 9 Mistakes – I've Made a Few   63

Chapter 10 How to format your EBook   64

Chapter 11 Get Crackin'   67

MAKE YOUR PAPERBACK 4 FREE

Chapter 1 Why Publish a Paperback?

I'm going to show you how to publish market and distribute your paperback for free, right here on Amazon! Like Clint Eastwood, for a few dollars more ($ 25), you can put it on the shelves of the major bookstores. Getting the book in print can be done for free.

Before we begin I want to say that, for your ease of reading I have chosen to publish this book in what's known as a "block text format" used in text books. It's used in situations where you have to look back and forth between the book and the computer screen and helps you keep track of where you are on the page.

I'm almost embarrassed to write this chapter. Of course you know why you want to publish your paperback. Notice I say, *almost* embarrassed.

There is more to know about this than meets the eye. The first thing people think about when it comes to publishing is the time and money it takes.

Bear with me for a very few pages while I share my frustrating past life. After that the sun breaks through the gloom and it gets downright cheery, honest. Yours can be looking up as well.

Contrary to the old saying, time is NOT money. If you're like me, you have a lot more time than money. Most people's first real effort goes, not into writing the novel, but, into finding a publisher.

MAKE YOUR PAPERBACK 4 FREE

In times past you could send a manuscript to a publisher and if they liked it, they would cut you a deal. Imagine how surprised I was when I discovered that times have recently changed.

Publishers don't accept manuscripts any more. They throw them away along with the junk mail. In fact, they have actually become the publisher's new junk mail. If you want a rejection letter, you have to put a self-addressed and stamped envelope (SASE) in with the "query letter". Sometimes I think they even eat the SASE.

The world's thirst for books has given way to video and audio entertainment to the extent that people just don't read the way they did in times past.

Now the writers just about outnumber the readers for a change and the publishing industry is getting mighty fussy. You can't swing a dead cat without hitting another want-to-be-author.

Publishers require you to have an agent. It's the agent who submits your work to the publisher, not you. I've contacted hundreds of agents. They are a snooty lot.

Never had one even agree to look at my book. They look at you over their eyeglasses, resting near the tip of their nose, their hair in a tight little bun, and ask, "Have you ever published a novel before?"

Unless you have a "platform" most agents and publishers will shun you.

Remember when people would go job hunting and the prospective employer would ask if you have experience? Even if you're trained, No experience, no job.

It's become the same in the publishing world. If you don't have a track record and followers, they won't hire your book. They want you to provide them with a ready-made customer base. Hey! I thought that was their job.

I have spent hundreds of hours building my platform (My ready-made customer base). I made several web sites. Every time I had a new commercial license in a new profession, I would build my web site. I even have one today http://WWW.robstetson.com and it doesn't help that much.

People don't go there because they know you. They know you because they go there. Why didn't the people who don't know you go there? Most people never heard about it, that's why. It's a vicious cycle.

If you listen to the experts, you will spend the next five years and hundreds, if not thousands, of dollars building that platform. Then all you'll have is a platform, not a book deal.

I have been published and was paid for thirteen original design articles in four major worldwide journals and magazines. No one cares.

A platform is made up of milestones called "planks" that are nothing more than black holes where your time goes funneling down into nowhere. I'll never get that time back.

So you're on the computer for hours at a time communicating with chatty commentators from all over the country, numbering from the tens to the hundreds.

You spend other nights and days talking to several thousand Twitter "followers" or hundreds of Facebook "friends" about everything in general and nothing in particular.

The whole thing strikes me as a form of reverse stalking. I call it reverse sucking. You pull them through your life behind you, talking about their vacation plans and their kid's school projects.

After looking at the photos of the 439th ugliest brats, you still haven't sold one book. You start to feel like a candidate kissing babies.

I'll tell you a secret about marketing your book. The quickest way to clean out your Facebook, Twitter and other assorted blogs is to start telling them about your book. People will disappear and your Email will dry up overnight. Nobody wants to hear about your unpublished book.

The same people who tell you to build a platform warn you not to try and sell your book to people you meet because it will annoy them. A sales pitch from someone you have just met is a turn-off, and even if you gain their full support, they aren't agents and can't get you published.

They think the only reason you befriended them was to sell them something. Well, I say, "It's time to stop the phony friend-gathering, get back to writing and get a life."

The platform does serve a purpose, don't get me wrong. It's creating the platform before you publish your first book that's a waste of time. It's like filing flight plans for your next 12 annual vacations before you look into the cost of getting a private pilot's license. You're not going anywhere.

Now this story gets more cheerful, my friend. Take back your life. I have my morning coffee now as the sun streams through the glass onto my morning paper. I am relaxed. I

MAKE YOUR PAPERBACK 4 FREE

am contented. I go now to my computer where I check my Email.

It's Email from my *REAL* friends, not my eight hundred Facebook friends. I start to work on my book and I love it. When I'm done with the book, I spend about a week spiffing it up and click on the publish button, then "holy moly!" my book has an ISBN and give it another week, I can order actual hard copies of my book for about $ 5 to $ 6 each.

My friend's eyes bug out in disbelief. The cover is gorgeous. They're slapping me on the back and buying me beers and talking about how they wish they could get their book into print.

Do you know what's really sweet? I can tell them how.

The victory isn't hollow. Any bookstore can order my book if it's not on their shelf. Anywhere in the world, you can buy my book. They can buy your book too.

Once you get your book published on Amazon, there are things you can do that begin your platform. Now your platform begins to serve a purpose.

Get a book finished on Amazon and available to sell in the book stores first.

Enough idle chat. Let's go to work here.

Chapter 2 Amazon as a Self-Publisher

After reading my book, if you can find a better paperback book deal, then go for it. I have scoured the Internet doing Google searches and reading between the lines. I can pay a fortune to get a book in my hands, but there won't be any payback.

The other publishers usually insist that they edit your book before they print, they don't actually publish books. They sell the thrill of seeing your book in print. Not for me! I'm in business to make a buck and so are you.

Most "vanity" presses are a rip-off. Not so with Amazon! Amazon publishes your book in paperback with a strikingly beautiful cover. They assign an ISBN for free, or you can pay them for an ISBN if you want to preserve some exclusive rights. I trust them. I do the exclusive deal for free.

They partner with you, taking your book-child under their wing and growing it into a mature market offering. It's like being married to a partner who can't nag you. Once the deal is signed and executed, they never ask anything more of you except where to mail your check. Is that love?

Just like a good solid marriage, I never have to worry about cheating. I find that Amazon is honest and totally upfront. I have peace of mind as I sit in front of my computer totally engrossed in my next masterpiece.

Some people want to touch the paper checks that come in the mail. Amazon will mail you a check. You can also have them deposit your royalties directly into your checking or savings account. As for me, my bank is burdened with the arduous task of processing my winnings for me. I'm just too busy writing my next book.

Amazon calls it "Create Space". Create space where? Create space for what? I think they must have been trying to keep it a secret. I would have called it "Publish your hard copy book for free". I might have even called it, "Let us put your hard copy book on the bookshelves of every major book retailer in the world". My ideas for naming the thing won't fit on a button smaller than the screen.

If you're going to be working in Create Space, you will need JavaScript and cookies.

Don't know if you have JavaScript? Log onto;

http://WWW.RobStetson.com and if you see menus on the left side of the screen, you have Java. If you see my menus, you can just exit my web page unless you want to stay a while and visit.

If you don't see my menus, that's no problem. Just click on the "Java Installer" link on the right side of my screen and follow the prompts to install it.

There! Now you have Java.

Now Log onto;

https://www.createspace.com/

You will be greeted by a sign in screen like this;

MAKE YOUR PAPERBACK 4 FREE

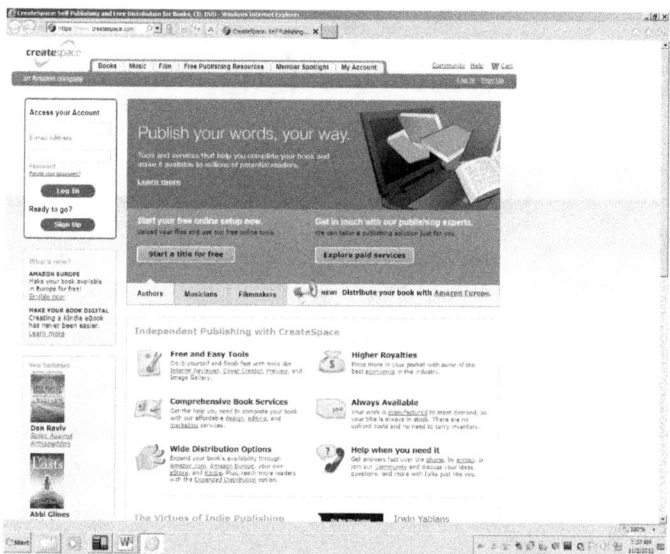

If you're reading this book, you obviously don't have an account on Create Space.

Under the Sign In button there is a button that says "Sign up". Click on that button.

As you create your account make sure the username and password are something you'll remember. In the event you forget your password, Create Space will Email it to you on request.

Now follow the instructions on creating your account, and then click on the Create My Account button. The screen should look something like this;

MAKE YOUR PAPERBACK 4 FREE

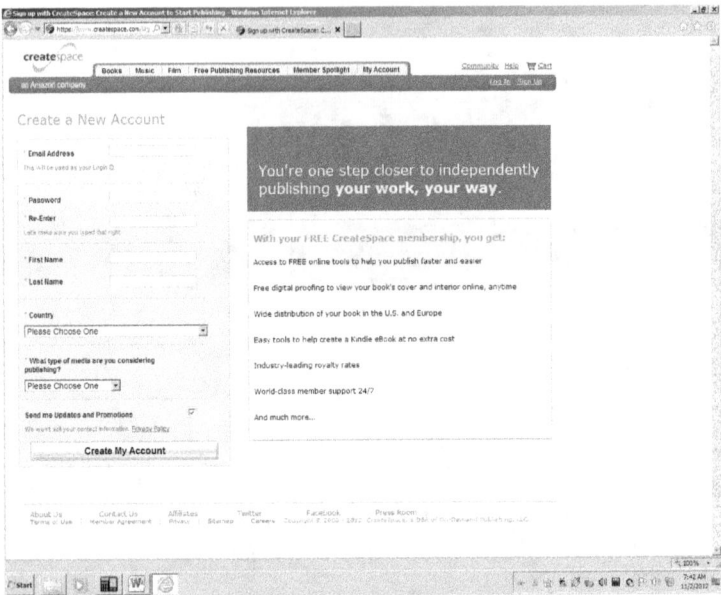

You're ready to start your new project. Your account information is maintained under your Email Address with a password.

When you fill out the registration screen you have to enter your password twice, in case you make a typographical error. Make sure you have a password you can remember.

You'll be going into this account frequently over the next few days or weeks at the least to get your book ready to publish.

Once you establish a Create Space login screen, it would be a good idea to put the login page for Create Space in your Internet Explorer or other browser Favorites menu.

The screen looks something like the one below;

MAKE YOUR PAPERBACK 4 FREE

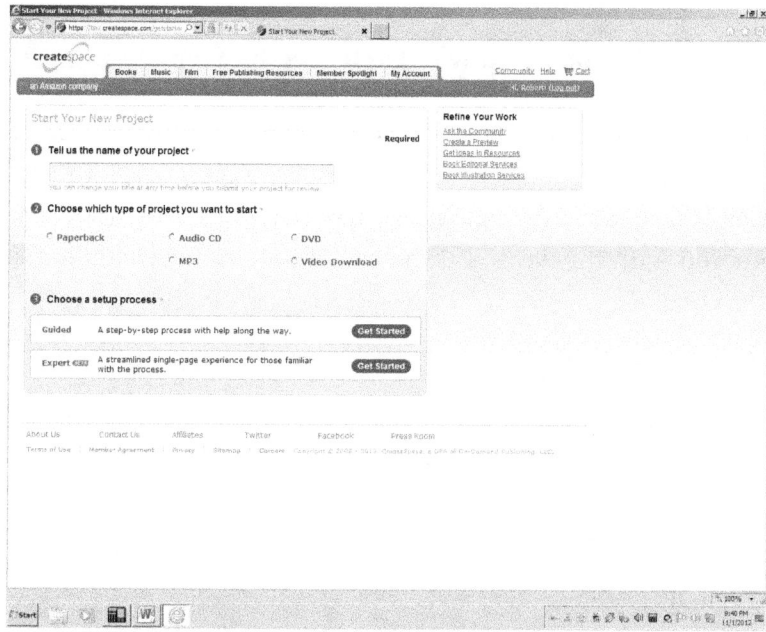

I'm assuming that your first project is a paperback. So click on the bullet marked paperback. Put the name of your book, or EBook in the "Tell us the name of your project" box.

Don't be a hero. Click on the Guided "get started" button. I clicked on the Expert button once and unless you know exactly how to dress all your files up in HTML before you even begin you won't get far.

The guided setup does all the conversions for you. I love it. Even if you know how to prepare the HTML, it's just more convenient to allow Amazon to walk you through the process of uploading and checking your Microsoft Word .Doc file.

MAKE YOUR PAPERBACK 4 FREE

Chapter 3 How to Do It Step by Step

If you don't mind doing some work, you can do it for free. I typically upload and correct and upload again three to five times before it comes out error free. If you don't want to be bothered with the work, I'll show you how to pay them to do it for you.

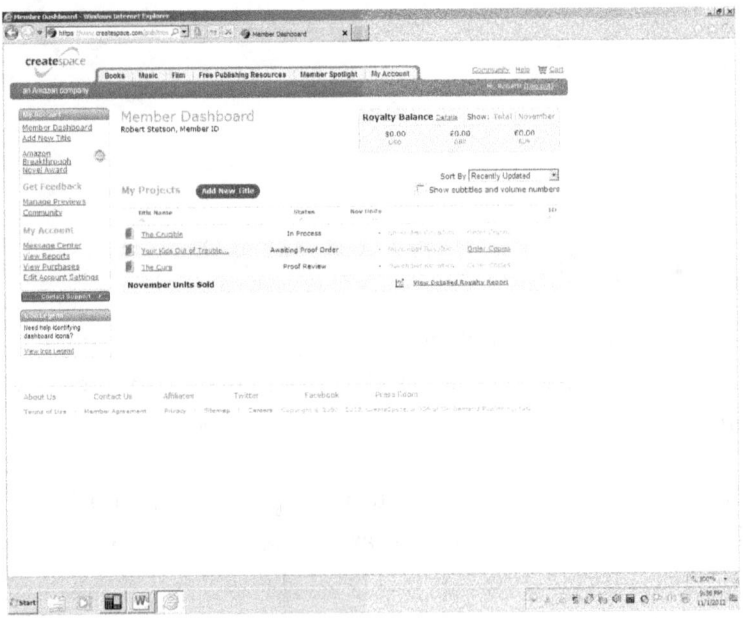

Now you're on what they call, "The Dashboard". All the online publishers I've seen seem to call this the Dashboard. It's become a generic term for the starting point in develping your book. The screen shown above is Amazon's Paperback Dashboard.

If you're ready to convert your book to their PDF format, then click on "New Book". The "Project Home Page" will appear. The screen shown below has five separate blocks. All of the red circles will have to turn green before you are finished. If you're doing it for FREE, you only have the three middle blocks to deal with.

I have enlarged the blocks in the Project Home Page to show the five areas of interest.

This is by far the best method for monitoring the process of paperback publishing that I have seen yet. When all the dots are green, your book is published, priced and distributed.

Let's break these red dots down down block by block.

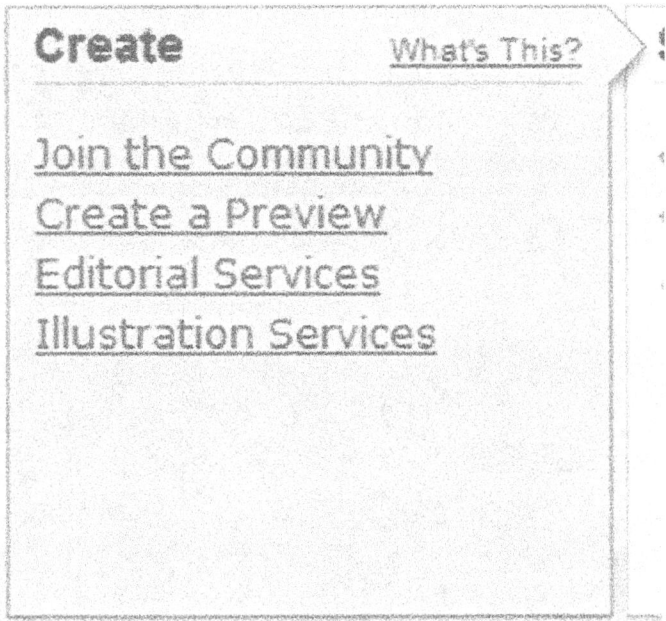

I'm not going to waste you time by going into great detail with each of the CREATE menu items. Come back to these and explore them on your own. If you're going to publish your book on your own, these menu items won't get your book uploaded.

1. Join the Community is the Blog area for their paperback publishing.

2. Create a Preview allows you to post previews and reviews for your book.

3. Editorial Services hire help to publish. Get pro services here if needed.

4. Illustration Services hire help for pictures. Pro services here if needed.

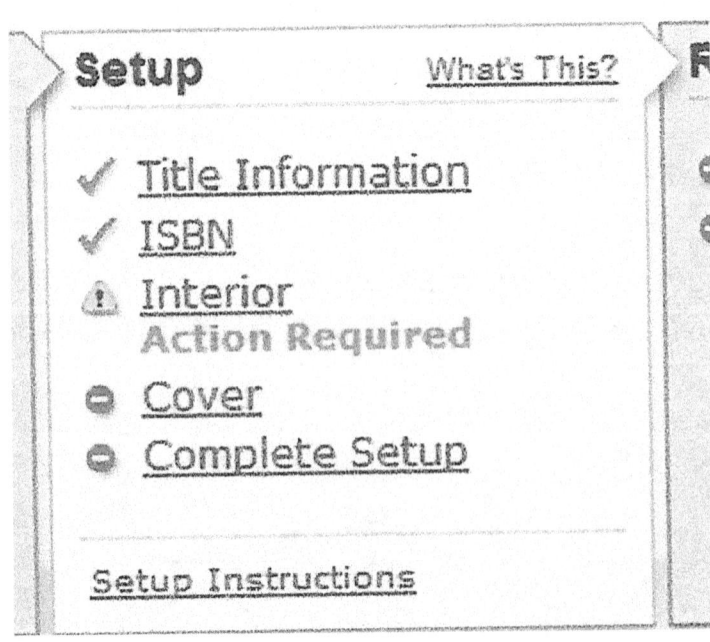

MAKE YOUR PAPERBACK 4 FREE

This is the Setup Information screen where you will actually create your book. It has five areas that must be completed to continue toward your goal. This block is the "meat and popato" section of the site. It's the 5 items needed to process your book. Let's take a look at the list of items we'll have to complete.

In the SETUP block, we have Five-Red dots when you begin. I have put up a SETUP block with three different status flags. The green check mark means that the item is completed.

The "Yellow Bang" will have a note under it in orange to indicate the reason for the yellow flag. Until this item is a green dot, the book will not be released for sale.

A Red-Dot with a minus sign indicates that the item is incomplete and needs to be answered before the book can be released.

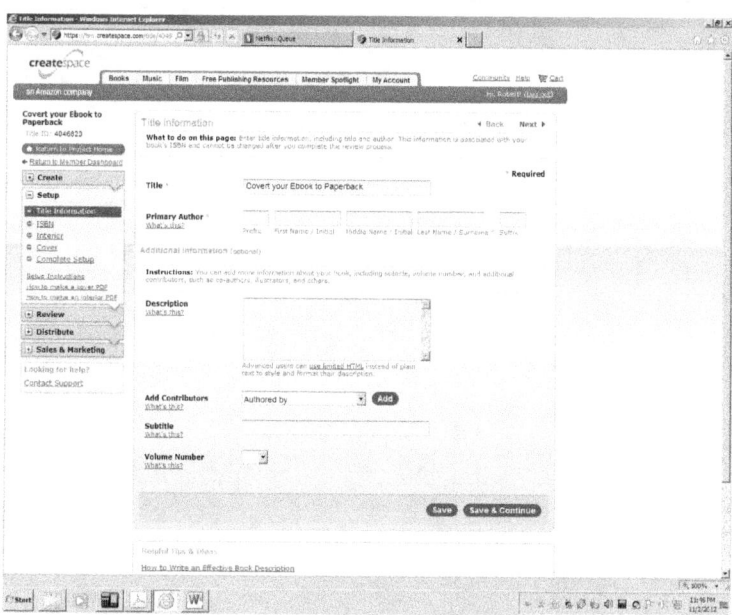

The "Title Information" selection will take you to the above page, where you enter the book title, your name and a description (Synopsis) of the book contents.

CAUTION: Don't get the "add authors" name entry mixed up with the "Primary Author" (your name) area. If you're the only author, leave add authors spot blank.

If your book has a sub-title, then enter it. Most books don't have a subtitle.

If your book is a volume in a series, put the volume number in the box provided, otherwise leave it blank. If there is no number in the box, the program will ignore this entry.

When you're done, obviously click on "Save and Continue". I'm not sure why you would want to just "Save". When you're done your next move will be to continue to the next block, even if you decide close the screen and log out at this point.

MAKE YOUR PAPERBACK 4 FREE

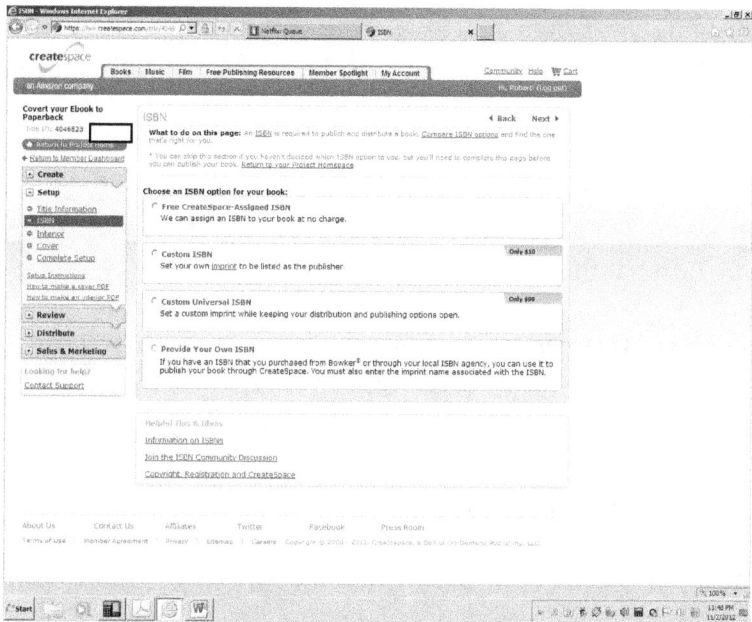

This screen in very important. You will only get to fill it out once, because once an ISBN number is assigned, it can't be changed or reassigned in the future. Let's take a look at the options available for assigning these numbers. I have included a short tutorial on how the numbers work and what they are. If you're reading this on a computer or EBook, you will have the option of skipping over the tutorial portion of this chapter.

If you select "Free Create Space", you are assigning the book to Create Space. This is good if you anticipate confining your business with regard to this book to Amazon. I like this idea.

The "custom ISBN" assigns you as the publisher, rather than Amazon. That's a $ 10 charge (You pick up the tab as Publisher).

The "Custom Universal ISBN" gives you the ability to keep your options open. You control your distribution. This is a $ 99 charge. "Freedom isn't free".

MAKE YOUR PAPERBACK 4 FREE

The "Provide your own ISBN" will allow you to plug in your pre-existing ISBN, assuming you already have one. In this case since you already own your ISBN, Amazon imposes no Charge.

If you're not interested in the inner workings of ISBN or ASIN numbers, you can skip ahead. Most people don't understand what these are or what they're for.

Now we're getting serious. Let's talk about the ISBN International Standard Book Number using the 13 Digit "Bookland Country Code".

If you don't care about all the irrelevant nitty-gritty details about the way the ISO, the ISBN or the ASIN works AND YOU ARE ON A computer, click on this link, **otherwise read on.**

Before the industry converted to the 13 digit code on January 1, 2007, the ISBNs were 10 digits. For example, ISBN-10: 1480220434

ISO (International Standards Organization) Standard TC46/SC9 is responsible for ISBN. The ISO on-line facility only goes back as far as 1978.

An ISBN is the unique identifier assigned to every book.

The ISBN is printed above the bar code on the back of the book in the lower right hand corner.

ASIN stands for Amazon Standard Item Number. Every product in Amazon's catalog has a unique 10-digit ASIN which Associates use when they want to link to that specific item on Amazon.com.

MAKE YOUR PAPERBACK 4 FREE

Don't confuse the ASIN (**A**mazon **S**tandard **I**dentification **N**umber) with the ISBN (**I**nternational **S**tandards **B**ook **N**umber). The ASIN assigned to a book is an Amazon unique identifier.

The ASIN for my book, "The Crucible" is B009FUA1KK.

You can find "The Crucible" on Amazon at http://www.amazon.com/dp/B009FUA1KK/

Let's break down the ISBN into its component parts, for example, let's use ISBN-13: 978-1-48-022043-0

ISBN-13: Denotes use of the Bookland country code.

The component parts are divided up a little differently than the standard format. I don't know why, but let's regroup the number for dissection i.e. 978-14-8022-043-0

The Bookland country code breaks down this way.

The first three digits "GS1" prefix identifies the Industry. <u>978</u> is for the book publishing industry.

The "Group Identifier is the language-Sharing Country Group. This is the next two numbers <u>14</u>.

The next four digits is the Publisher Code. For Amazon that's <u>8022</u>.

The "Item Number" <u>043</u> denotes the title.

The "Checksum" or Parity Check <u>0</u> is the last digit.

An International Standard Book Number consists of those 5 parts:

MAKE YOUR PAPERBACK 4 FREE

Now it's time to get back to the business of building your book.

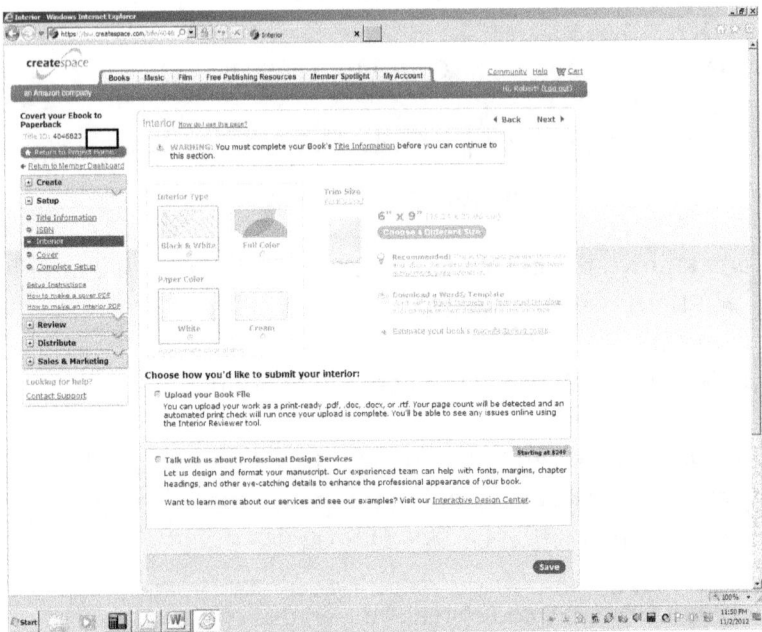

I would strongly recommend you not start this process unless you have finished writing your book and have it ready to go in MS Word format.

If we had a book all formatted and ready to upload, we would do it here, so let's stop here and I'll show you step by step how to make your book ready to upload into this page.

If you want to have your document ready to upload as an EBook, then click Chapter 10 How to format your EBook.

How to Format Your Paperback

If you're ready to do the paperback then stay on this page and continue. I will show you how to format your MS Word

.doc and put in the headers, footers, menu and other bells and whistles. You will need to trim up the document as required to correct errors when you upload it.

In order to get the book to work properly, you need a "print ready" file. Be sure and save any book pages as a ".doc" file. Don't attempt to do it with a "docx" file. You can specify the ".doc" file format when saving the document using "save as" rather than "save".

Don't let the words "print ready" scare you. It's all done for you and if there is an issue, I'll explain exactly how to fix it. It's simple to do.

Chapter 4 Formatting your Book with MS Word

Use MS Word 2010 to create your book pages and then you can cut and paste the text from the MS Word document to the template. When you have completed the transfer of all your pages, you have a "book Ready document.

If you need to see what is needed in the leading pages of your book, take a look at this one. The lead in pages should be the same with the EBook format, except for the ISBN numbers. EBooks don't require ISBN Numbers, but if I have an ISBN from a previously published paperback I put it on the leading page of the EBook.

Don't forget to put the copyright notice up front as well. It's the traditional place for it. If they don't see the copyright notice, they (they being the readers) will assume you don't have any property rights with regard to the document contents.

Now you're almost ready to upload the word document into the upload page, but not quite.

EBooks don't have headers, footers or page numbers. Whether you're document source is a previously published EBook or a new document, you will have to add these.

With a paperback book, every time you make a change in the font, style or other attributes, the pagination will change. Adding headers and footers can also change the pagination.

One of the most common mistakes new authors make is that by the time they finish tweaking the book content, they forget to repaginate the Table of Contents. I'll be sure and remind you later.

By the way... Did you right justify your text and menu? A professional looking book has smoothly aligned left and right edges. The "ragged edge look" is considered highly amateurish. That goes for printed books and EBooks alike.

Let's talk about how the headers, footers and page numbers should look.

If you select a header and page number combination that appear on or near the outside edge of the pages, make sure they are on the correct edge of the page, else they will be near the inside (gutter) of the page.

This is where it gets hairy. I want to warn you that the whole thing about reviewing the pages on Amazon is somewhat counterintuitive. After all the effort to place the headers and footers toward the left on the left page and toward the right on the right page, when you review it in the reviewer, they will be reversed. The left page will have the header and footer on the right and the right page will have the header and footer on the left. This is both normal and correct.

The first page is always a right hand page, but being the first page, the header and footer starts on the left.

One easy way to sidestep the entire right and left format issue is to select a header and footer format that is centered on the page.

When you're doing the headers and footers, be sure and check the headers and footers of both the odd and even pages, as they need to both be present. Some headers and footers are separately assigned to odd and even pages.

Page numbering is automatic. You should start numbering on the first page of the first chapter with "1, 2, 3", etc. The first section of the book from the title page through the Introduction should be numbered "i, ii, iii". You can fix the document to have a first page without the number being displayed. Whether the number on the first page is being displayed or not, the title page (first page) is always counted as page i.

I always put the ISBN 10 and the ISBN 13 numbers on the first page; it's just the way I do things. I want people to know the book is not only copyrighted, but that the copyright is registered with the copyright office.

The table of Contents is different for a printed book than they are for an EBook. For an EBook you never use page numbers because the font selection changes the words per page and the chapters, pages and flags are based on the hyperlink locations. In a printed book, there are no hyperlinks, but the page content is obviously fixed. When you go to the "references" tab on your word document, always select page numbers right justified when building your table of contents.

One of the things that make EBooks easier is that they don't require pagination. One of the most common mistakes new authors make is that by the time they finish tweaking the book content for the paperback, they forget to recreate the Table of Contents.

Make sure when you create the table of contents that you go to the "References" tab in MS Word and click on "Table of Contents". If you've never made a table of contents before, you have to go to the bottom of the menu that drops down and click on "Insert table of contents".

A paperback table of contents is different from an EBook table of contents. In the paperback table of contents you have to check the "Show Page Numbers" and you can leave the "Use Hyperlinks instead of page numbers" option set. The hyperlink option will not change the appearance of the menu and will allow you to more speedily navigate the book when editing.

When you select the Page Number option, make sure you set the "Right Justify" option.

When you set up the Menu, make sure you select only the types of headers you will be using. The "Show Levels" automatically comes up with three levels. Unless you have sub-headers or sub-sub-headers, change the number of headers to "1".

Don't be concerned about the hyperlink usage. The hyperlink blue print along with the characteristic underline is not visible even though they are hyperlinks.

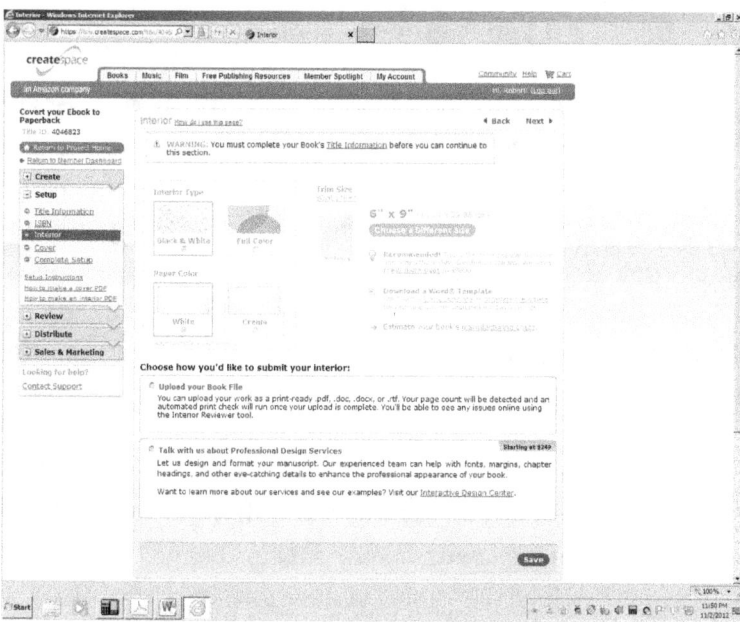

When you're ready, click on the "Interior" tab on the left side of the Create Space screen and the page above will appear.

Near the bottom of the page are the boxes labeled "Choose how you'd like to submit your interior"; I prefer to do it for FREE, and after all, isn't that why we're here? Click on the bullet for "Upload your Book File".

The "Interior" screen is where you upload your book pages. The default dimensions of the finished book are 6" by 9". Unless you know exactly how to proceed without help, don't change the trim size. You will soon see why.

The 6" by 9" form factor is the standard Amazon book size. I recommend it because it's larger and easier to hold and read than the old "Dime Novel" size, yet it's smaller than a full sized book.

------- Caution. Don't paste into the template yet --------
------ until I tell you it's time to choose your options ----

There are two links for downloading a template to use with MS Word. I'm not going to assume that you're uploading an EBook, but if you are, just jump forward to the point where we cut and paste our book into the template. If you don't have a book document yet, continue on without clicking on the link. If you already have a book document ready for upload, then you are ready to cut and paste it into the template, but wait until I tell you it's time.

You can choose to download both the blank template and the formatted template, open each of them up and decide which you prefer to transfer your document to. Leave the one you like best and delete the other. Leave the one you like best open on the screen and open your book document.

MAKE YOUR PAPERBACK 4 FREE

------------Now decide on changes to the document.-------

I like to leave the document in the standard 8 ½" by 11" format and just upload it to the "upload your book file" page. The page will get an error and suggest that you are attempting to load a page that is 8 ½" by 11".

Here's where the magic happens. I had 8 errors when I uploaded it in the standard 8 ½" X 11" format because it wasn't in the 6" by 9" format. If you do that, then you are given the option of allowing Amazon to convert your 8 ½" to 11" document to the proper format for you! I said "yes" to allowing Amazon to convert the document for me and the document was created automatically. Then my 8 errors became 4 errors because the format size errors were automatically corrected. These 4 remaining errors were just small formatting issues. I fix them and now they're golden.

If you choose not to go the route I have taken, it's time to cut and paste manually.

Cut and paste the document into the template if you choose this route. If you choose this route, I prefer the blank template because all the deleting of the filler text is such a pain in the butt.

I'm going to repeat this process showing you how to navigate the screens through upload testing and editing. Let's take it step by step.

MAKE YOUR PAPERBACK 4 FREE

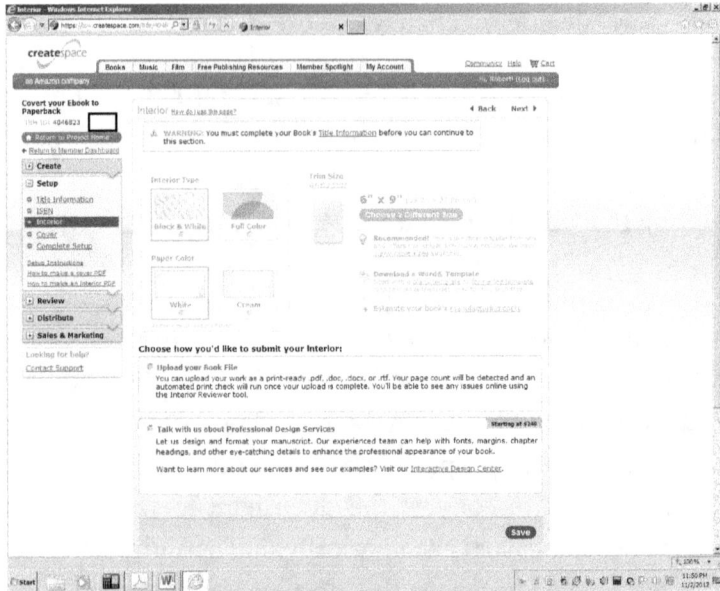

Whichever approach you chose, this is the "Interior" screen.

If your chapter headers are not set up as "Header 1" format and all the other regular text is not set up as "Normal" then do that now.

If you don't know the basics of using MS Word, then that is beyond the scope of this book.

MAKE YOUR PAPERBACK 4 FREE

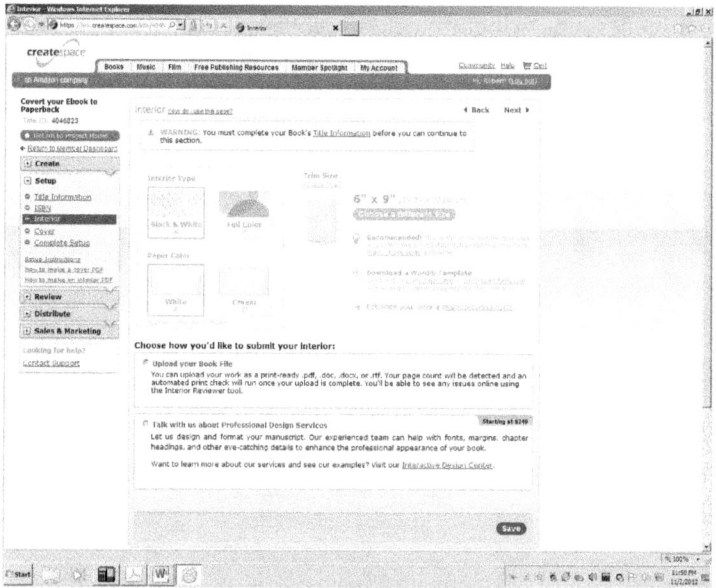

It's time to get to work formatting your book for the Amazon printer. Start by uploading your work in the above screen with the "Upload your Book File" button selected.

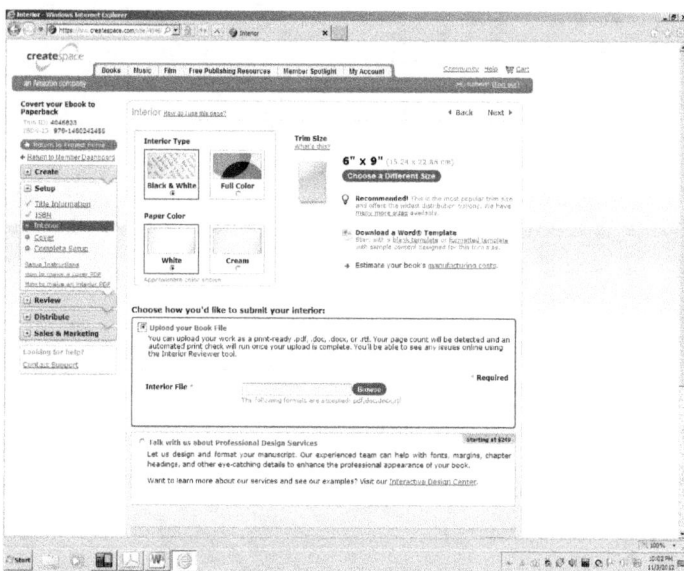

MAKE YOUR PAPERBACK 4 FREE

Now this screen appears and you are prompted for the Interior file. Click on the "Browse' button and find the directory where your file is located.

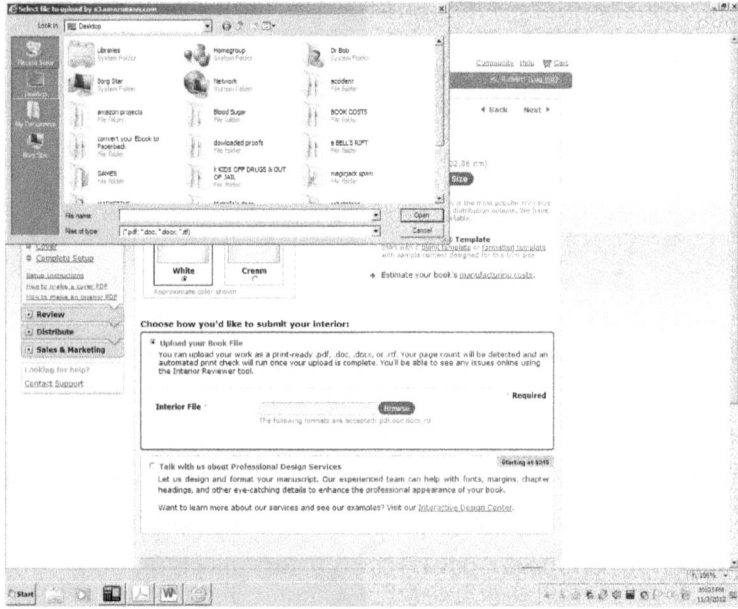

Locate your file in the directory and you can double click on it to select it.

MAKE YOUR PAPERBACK 4 FREE

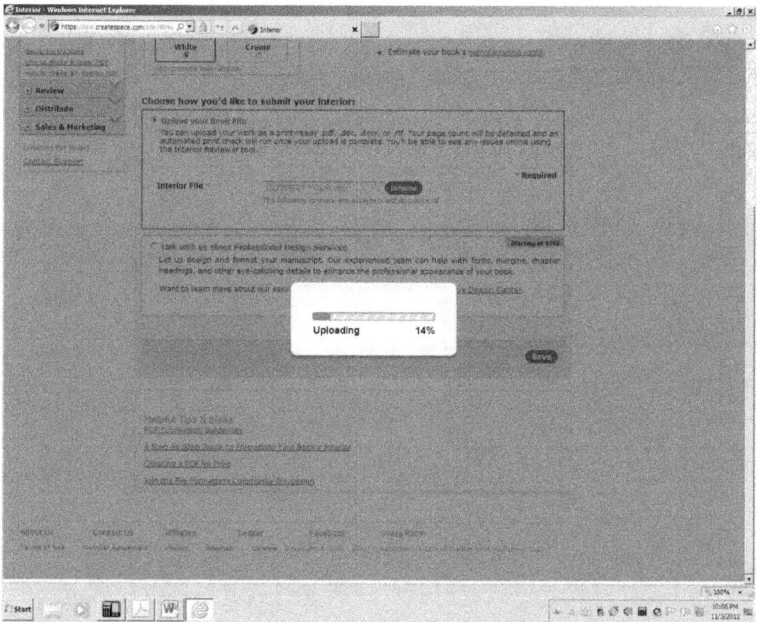

The file name will appear in the browse window. Run the screen scroll bar to the bottom. Now the "Save" button is visible. Press the save button and your file will begin to upload as shown in the screen above.

MAKE YOUR PAPERBACK 4 FREE

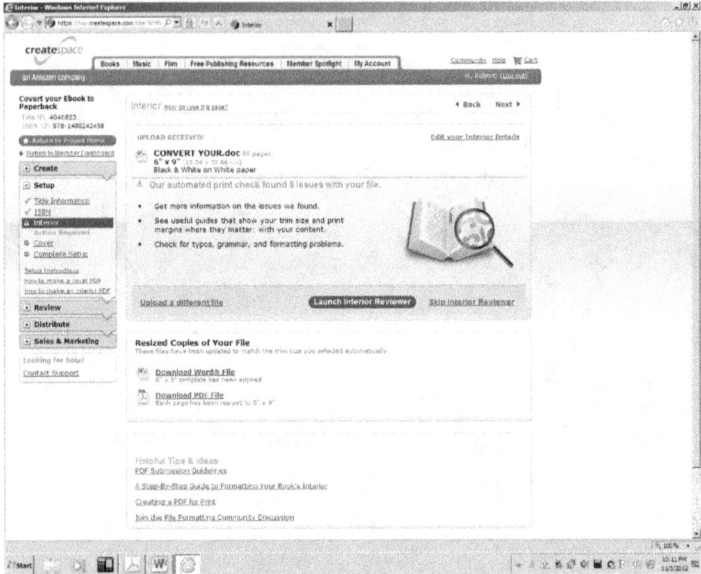

Next, the screen above will appear and you can expect to see a message in orange saying that "Our automated print check found (n) issues with your file".

Don't be discouraged, this is normal. We can fix the problems.

I deliberately uploaded a file with full sized pages rather than using their 6X9 template to show you that even if you ignore the template, the software will fix it for you. See the following screen shot.

MAKE YOUR PAPERBACK 4 FREE

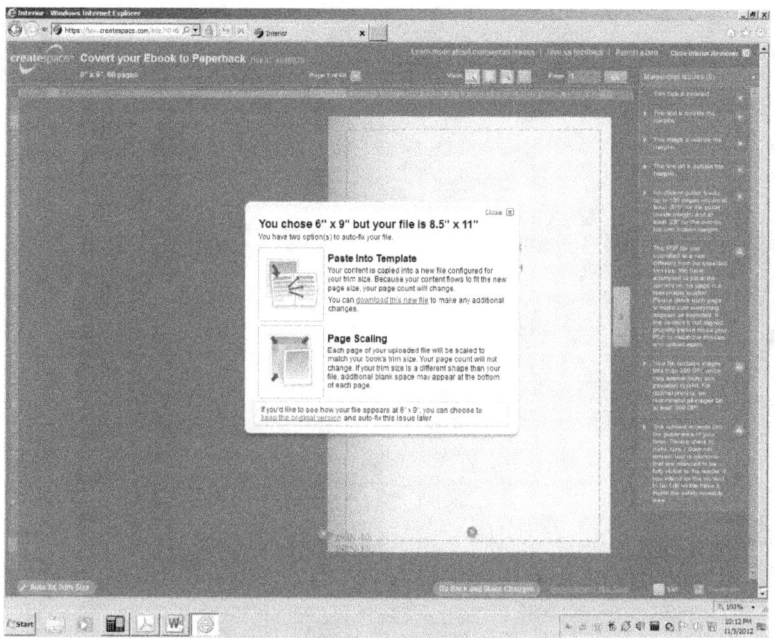

Just click on "download this new file". The new file will be named something like the following,

"Convert_your_Ebook_to-CSP_Size_Fix-11-04-12.doc".

This is a fix file and is the properly formatted version of the file you uploaded. You can rename this is you want, or leave it as is. This is the file you will adopt as your book for editing and uploading in the future.

MAKE YOUR PAPERBACK 4 FREE

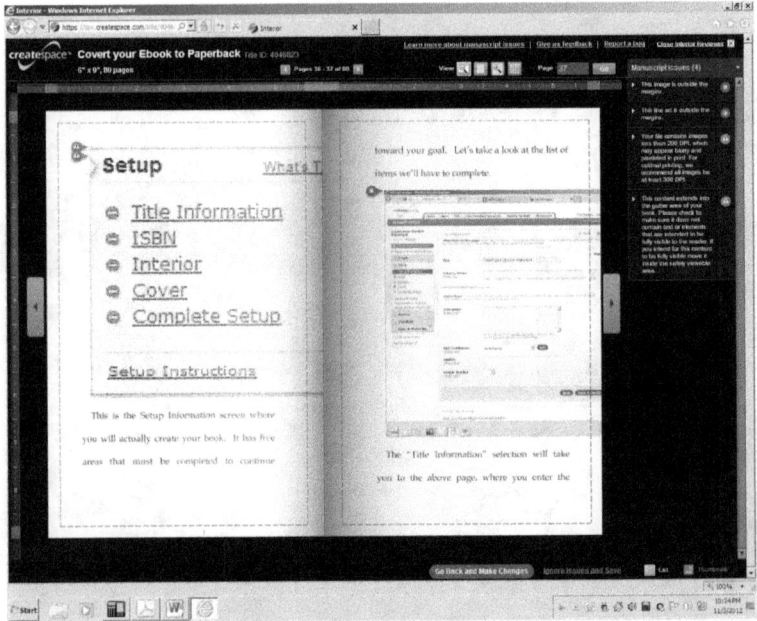

Just the act of allowing the Interior Previewer to autofix the file has resulted in a reduction from 8 errors to 4 errors.

On the upper right you have an explanation for each error, while if you locate the page or pages where the error occurred, it will flag the exact cause of the error by flagging the item you need to fix.

These errors are caused by the artwork extending beyond the margine on both the right page and the left page. I fixed the errors by shrinking the pictures in my MS Word document and then re-uploading the file.

References made to errors pertaining to the "gutter" area means the area where the left and right pages meet in the middle of the open book.

Thicker books over 600 pages require a larger gutter area because the pages don't spread as wide making it more difficult to see the inner areas of the text, so they leave more room in the gutter.

If you really care about the quality of your book, you will be uploading and tweaking it several times even after all the errors are fixed. I had to fuss with the headers, footers, gutters, etc. etc. I typically work a minimum of a week or two just fussing with the details in the page layout.

Let's imagine you have everything looking good. When you run the Internal Previewer, it will look like the screen shot below.

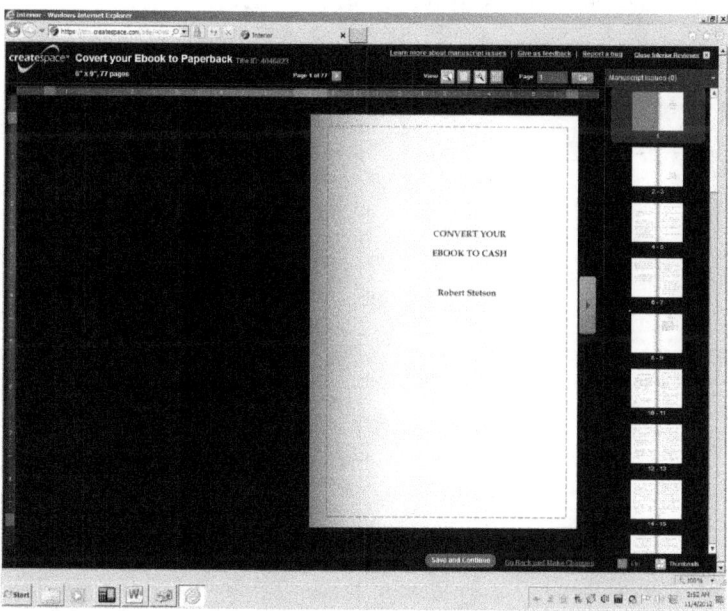

This is an error free document. The stream of pages on the right are thumbnails of the pages. It makes it easier to find photos and errors when you can go straight to the page.

Whenever you go to upload your document the software will invite you to work on your cover while you wait. I recommend that you DON'T DO THAT.

Stay focused on the element you're working on. Focusing on one item at a time my take a little longer, but it makes the job easier and keeps your mind clear with regard to the task at hand.

When you're happy with the results of your printed inner portion of the book, click on "Save and continue", otherwise click on the red words, "Go back and make changes". Rework the document, upload again and check it again, again and again.

Let's imagine the document is completely done. Now you can go forward and begin work on the cover.

Chapter 5 Building Your Cover

Some people think this is the easy part. I strongly recommend that you spend some quality time considering the look of the cover.

The old saying, "You can't tell a book by its cover" is somewhat misleading. A sloppy or ugly, or unreadable cover makes the whole book flop. People equate the appearance of the cover as reflecting on the quality of the overall project.

I'm going to say this again later in the book, because it's so true and it's so important. People don't read, they skim. If your cover and your title doesn't catch their eye, they will breeze right by your book in the lineup. You will lose sales.

It's true with movies as well. Have you ever seen a preview and were just blown away with the excitement it generated, only to see the movie and wonder how it could be so bad? I often thought they should make movies based on the preview, not the other way around.

Think of your cover as your preview. It really is.

Now down to business. You have a book to sell and I want you to finish it and make some quality money.

MAKE YOUR PAPERBACK 4 FREE

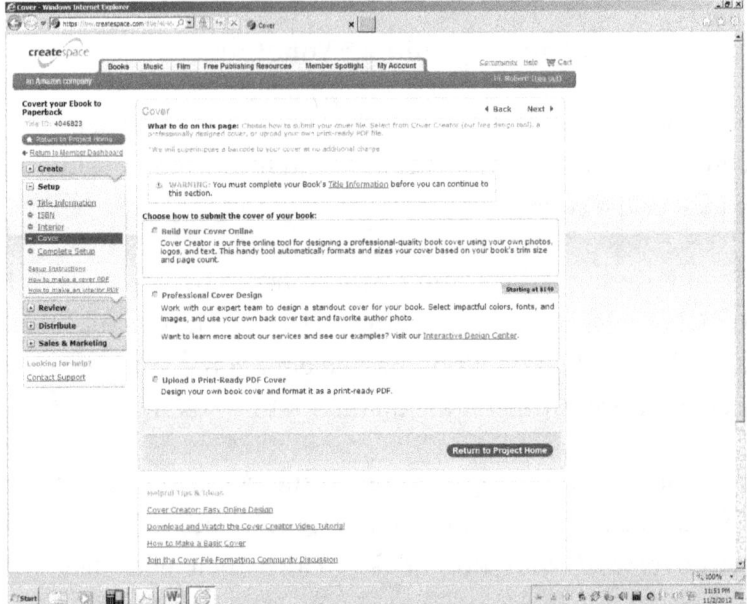

When you select "cover" in the "Create Menu" it will take you to the screen above. You have the option of "Building your cover online". This is the one we're going to choose, unless you decide to go with a paid cover design.

"Professional Cover Design" is among the options for those who decide they would rather have someone else do it for them.

You can also "Upload a Print Ready PDF Cover". I think Building your cover online is a perfectly good choice. If you decide to pay someone to do a cover after we're done, I'll be surprised. You can do a great job, I'm sure.

Click on "Build Your Cover Online".

MAKE YOUR PAPERBACK 4 FREE

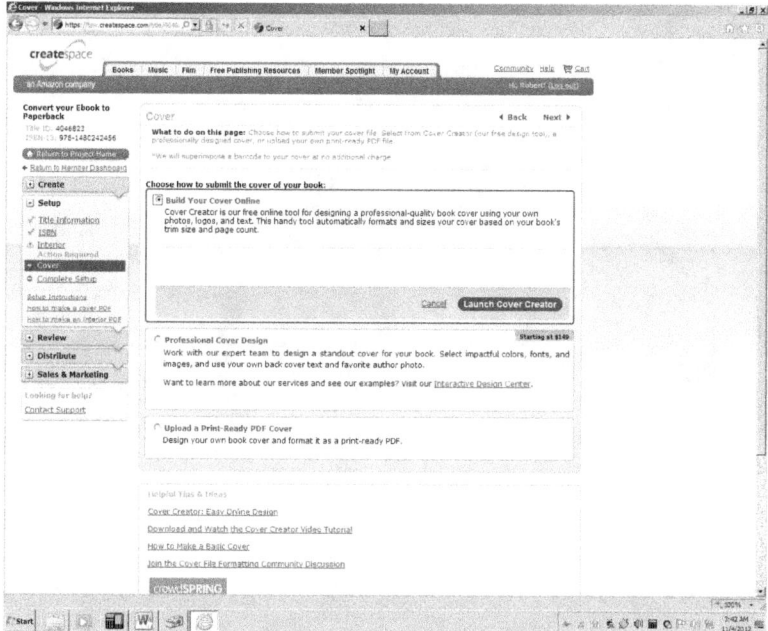

Now the box opens to enable you to "Launch Cover Creator". Click on the button to launch.

MAKE YOUR PAPERBACK 4 FREE

When you launch the cover creator you're confronted with the choice of various cover designs. I selected the Bonsai for my cover, I just like the looks of it and it has the best layout for this lind of book, but I don'e like the color green (yuk!). I'm also not fond of the picture. With cover creator I can fix both of these issues.

You can get pictures from an online public domain picture website, such as http://www.public-domain-image.com/, or you can use the pictures from this one. The photos on Amazon are excellent and they are public domain as well.

You will need a good copy of your photo to place in the Author's photo window. The photo will make you a real person in the eyes of the readers. It's a nice touch.

WARNING!!! DO NOT USE THE PHOTO FROM YOUR DRIVER'S LICENSE. Ha ha ha. Just kidding. The DMV is not the best source of photography.

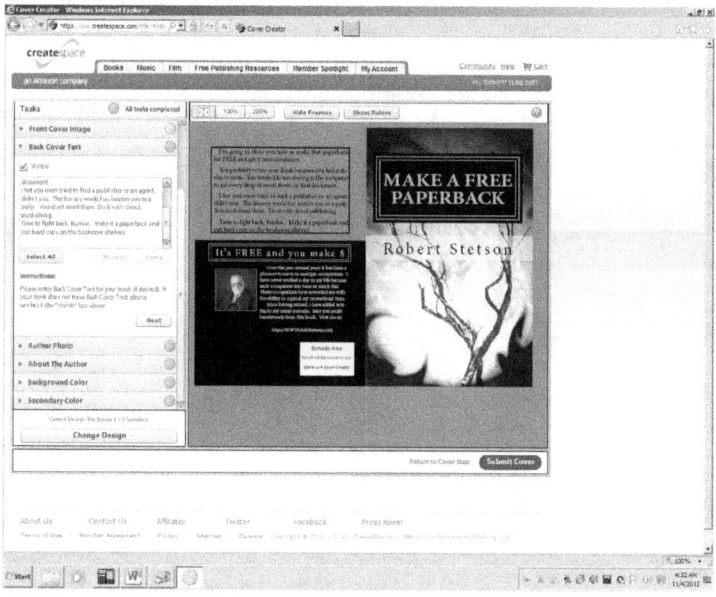

Write a synopsys of the book and place it in the area provided on the back of the book. This can be the same synopsis you have on your EBook, assuming you have an EBook on the Internet.

Now you have to do a piece "about the Author" to ut next to your picture. You can say just about anything you like in this spot. Make sure it's about you and something you don't mind sharing with the world.

Don't worry about the ISBN block on the lower right hand corner of the back cover. The publisher typically puts that there for you. It protects their investment in your book by warning the world not to copy it.

If there is anything you want to change later, such as the background color for instance, just restart the cover creator and choose the background color. A color chart will appear and you click on the background color you want. I chose "bright yellow" for the back cover and title colors. I want a cover so bright it makes you blink twice when you look at it.

Now the cover is done and you want to save it. Click on the "Complete Cover" button and you will get a full view of your handiwork. It's nice to know that your choices are never set in stone with this software. You can do anything but change the ISBN. The ISBN box will indicate that it is locked.

If you look at the cover you made and go "Yuck!" it's a simple matter to go back and change the entire appearance of the cover from scratch. The "Start a New Cover From Scratch" is not a button, but a link.

If you elect to make a smaller change, like the title, the background color or the artwork, then just click on "Edit Cover" and you can tweek the design.

MAKE YOUR PAPERBACK 4 FREE

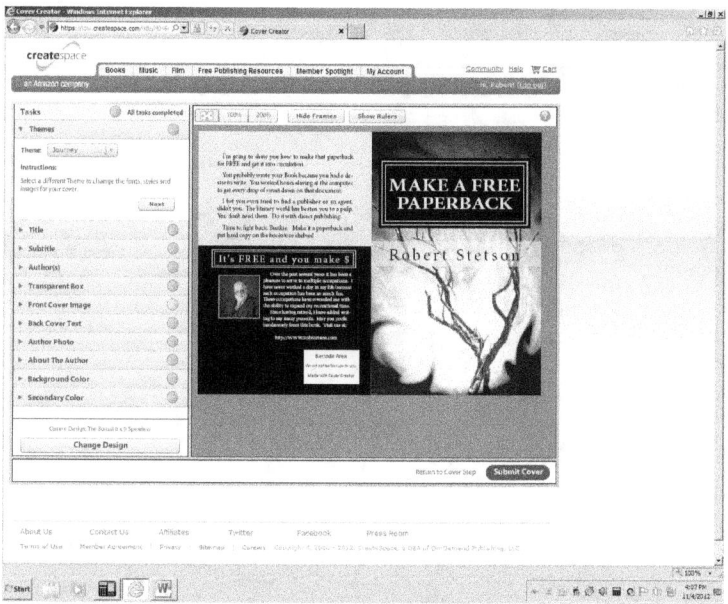

Here is a full view of the handiwork created in this demo. Just remember, this cover is mine. Just look at the outside of the book your reading. I'll et you can do as well or better.

If you're happy with the cover just press the "Submit Cover" button, but don't be nervouse. Until you submit their finished work for final approval yu can still go back and change anything, including the title.

One thing before you close on the cover. Make sure the name of the project, which you can also change, by the way, matches the title on the cover and the title in the document or the siftware will not allow you to submit it for final approval.

MAKE YOUR PAPERBACK 4 FREE

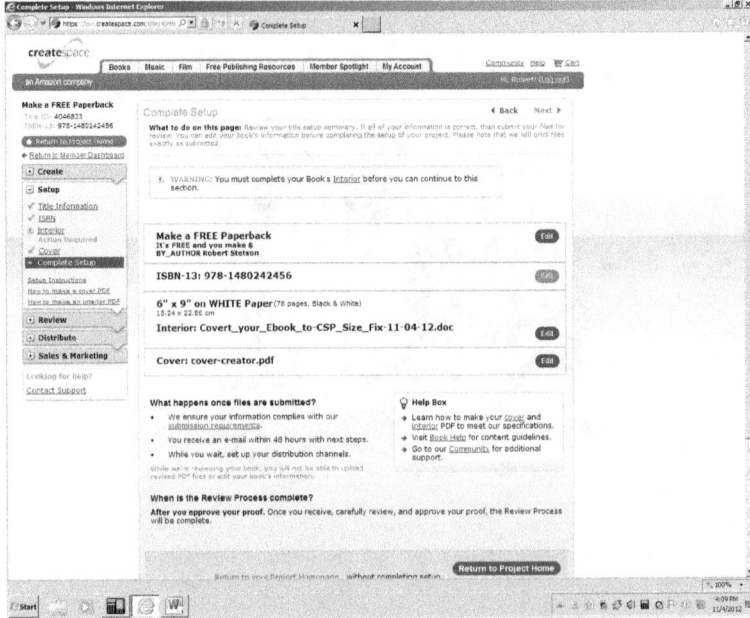

This is the "Complete Setup" screen. Notice the warning near the top of the screen. You must complete the interior (text portion) of the book before you are allowed to submit it for final approval. I'm obviously not done with the text portion of this book.

Ah the review screens. This means that you're almost done. Not so. Submit the interior text and the cover for review together when they are both done. Unless they are both completed error free the software won't let you submit the book for review.

They are not done until you have scrutinized them more than once. Read and reread the text. Ponder the cover. If you rush through the release process you will create delays when the reviewer discovers errors, such as the title on the document and the submission and the cover not all being the same, for example.

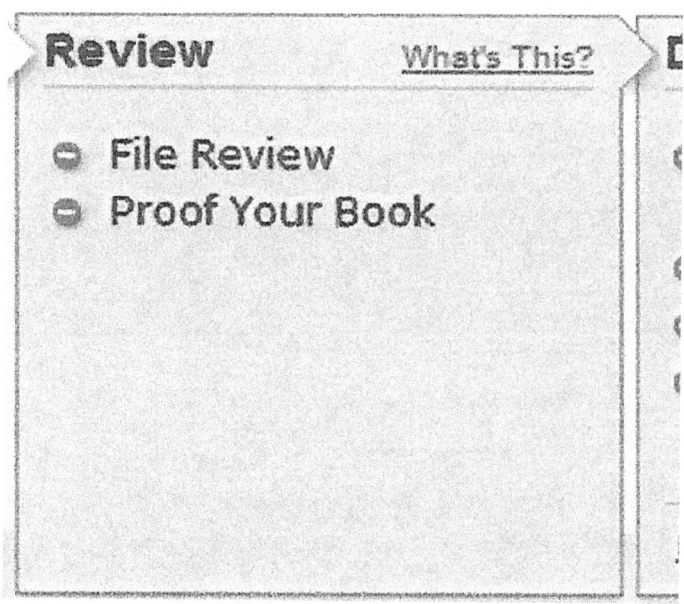

Even now, you can change any part of your book right down to the title and project name.

When the files have passed the review process you will be invited to proof your book.

Up to now it's all been about them approving your work, now the burden is on you to read and approve the work in the form of an author's PROOF. In the publishing industry, when you read and approve the proof, you are assuming full responsibility for the book. Typographical errors, factual errors, bad grammar, and any other kind of error now belong to you.

The publisher has one responsibility. The publisher must conform to your proof and produce a book that is manufactured to the best physical quality standards of the industry.

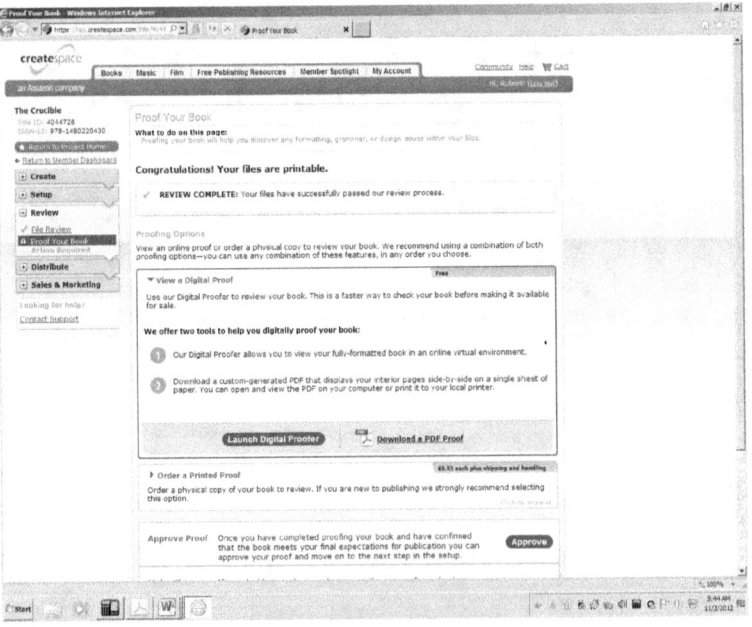

With my book, The Crucible I turned out a book I was very proud of. I know your book will be of the same quality.

MAKE YOUR PAPERBACK 4 FREE

Where can you get your book published and on the shelves?

You're home now, right here on Amazon.com.

Chapter 8 Paperback Marketing is Easy

> **Distribute** What's This?
>
> ⊖ **Channels**
>   6 more available (0 selected)
> ⊖ **Pricing**
> ⊖ **Description**
> ⊖ **Publish on Kindle**
>
> Distribute Instructions

With EBooks you have to shake the trees yourself, posting ads and spending endless hours hobnobbing on Twitter and Facebook.

On Amazon, if you elect to work the system for $25 you can be linked to all the major chains that will see your book emblazoned on their screens when their ordering books for the store.

In case you thought you were done, not so fast. You're a business professional now. Amazon is waiting for you to tell them what you want done for you. You have the job of being the CEO of your book selling industry. You have to decide what sales channels you're going to adopt.

Channels, you say? Are we on TV?

Channels are the paths you choose to sell your books through. Channels include distributors, retail and wholesale outlets and any other path your book will be sold through. EBooks are sold through the Internet download channel. Let's take a peek at the six channels offered by Amazon.

Sales and marketing are usually negotiable between the publisher and the writer. With most of the "vanity presses", the entire job of sales, distribution and marketing are in your lap. You will pay them handsomely for their services and you will be the only source for their orders. You will pound the pavement, dial the phone and have book showings all orchestrated by you alone. It's a lonely business and one that is doomed to failure.

With Amazon, you can rely on them to do all the mundane business of sales, distribution and marketing. Meanwhile, you can augment their efforts by doing as much of this as you want.

You can order your books wholesale (some of mine cost less than $4). Resell them at just above wholesale to bookstores. Resell them to the public at retail over the counter prices. With Amazon, your books will be sold whether you take an active role or not. Later on you will see how easy it is to boost your sales, but for now, let's look at the channels.

MAKE YOUR PAPERBACK 4 FREE

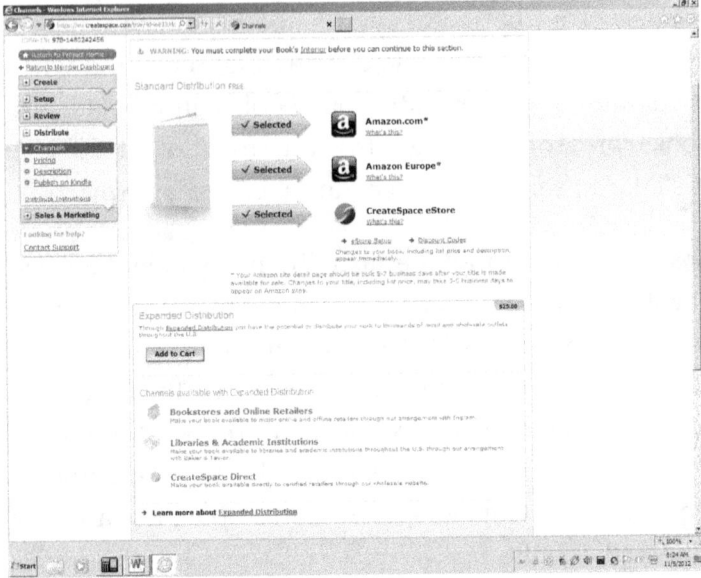

Six Channels of Distribution

Free channels include;

Your work is listed for sale on **Amazon.com,** where your books are listed for sale online in the Amazon.com Bookstore. If you have either an EBook or a paperback and you add the other, they are then both listed together in the store.

Your work is listed for sale on **Amazon.com Europe** and recently **Amazon.com Japan** as well, where your books are listed for sale online in the Amazon.com Bookstore.

Your work is listed for sale on the **Create Space eStore** but only if you set it up. Under the Create Space eStore there is a link labeled, "eStore Setup". Click on this link.

49

MAKE YOUR PAPERBACK 4 FREE

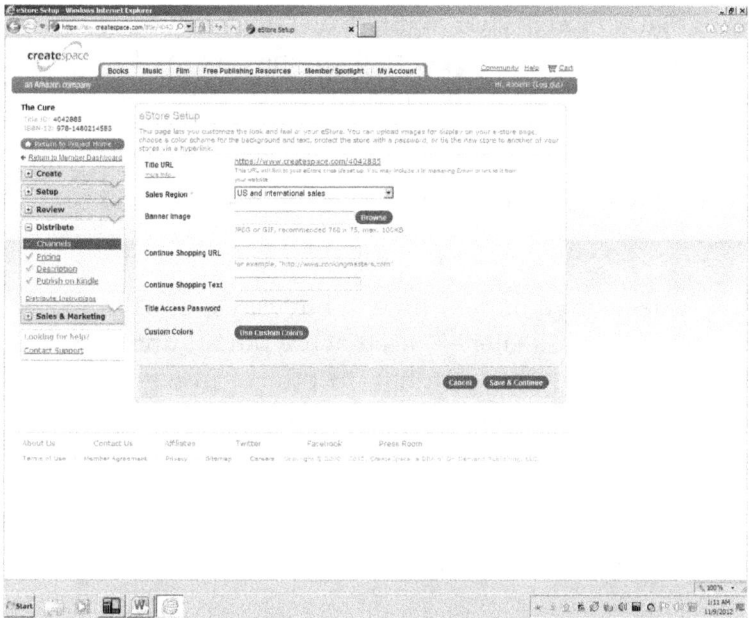

Now your eStore setup screen appears. Here you can create your own little website page featuring the book for which this channel is designated.

Each book gets its own dedicated eStore page, so every time you add a book to the dashboard, you need to come here and set up the eStore webpage for that book.

These are some of my eStore pages if you want to see how they look.

This is my webpage for THE CURE
https://www.createspace.com/4042885
This is my webpage for THE CRUCIBLE
https://www.createspace.com/4044728
This is my webpage for YOUR KIDS OUT OF TROUBLE & INTERNET SAFE
https://www.createspace.com/4044941

MAKE YOUR PAPERBACK 4 FREE

The next great option is your ability to create discount codes. When you're on the "Channels" page, click on the link marked "Discount Codes" to the right, next to the "eStore Setup" link.

Click on the Discount Codes link and the window below will open giving you the ability to create and define discount codes for your customers.

Discount codes with a limited time to buy can spur sales that might have been put off until later. Sales that are put off until later can fail to materialize, so if you're willing to offer a discount and take a smaller royalty for that sale, this is a useful tool.

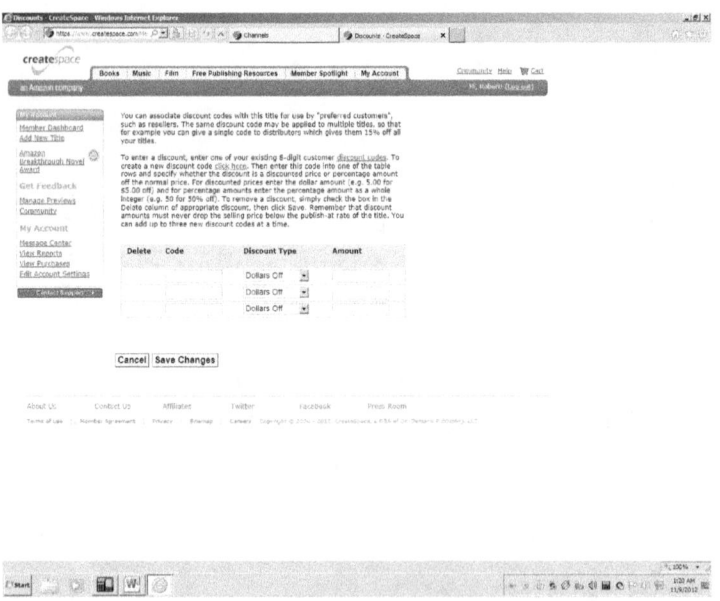

If you choose to pay the $25 fee for the expanded distribution, you will open up the screen below. You will need to select the three marketing channels in order to activate them after you pay the fee.

MAKE YOUR PAPERBACK 4 FREE

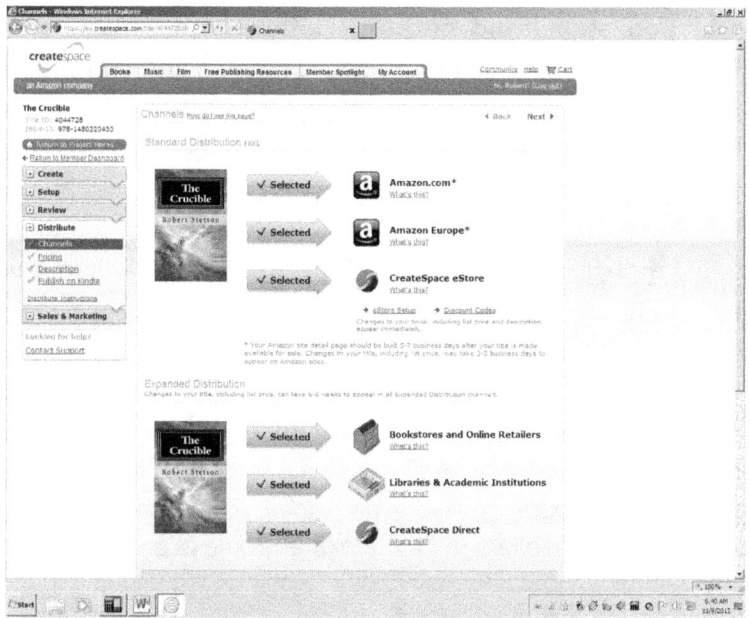

Yes, I know I said it's free to make your own paperback, but the paperback is made and **it is free**.

You are not obligated to spend the $25 and the book will be offered for sale through the first 3 channels at no cost to you.

Publishing the book is the responsibility of Amazon, but the cost of marketing the book <u>outside of Amazon</u> is your responsibility. The marketing offer made below by Amazon is a bargain. Don't pass it up!

If you want your books sold in bookstores like Borders or Tatnuck Booksellers, and more, you can wear out your shoe leather and visit all the booksellers around the world to sell your books.

As for me, I paid the $ 25.

For $25 more;

Sell to **Bookstores and online Retailers**. Amazon.com has direct sales channels to thousands of Bookstores and online retailers. Because Amazon.com has a reputation as a source of books in the industry, your book has a better than average chance of being in their sales inventory.

Sell to **Libraries and Academic Institutions** for their public or private library shelves. Sell to colleges and Universities for their college bookstores.

Sell through **Create Space Direct** where people can buy your paperbacks from certified resellers such as independent bookstores and book resellers participate in a direct program allowing eligible resellers to buy books at wholesale prices.

MAKE YOUR PAPERBACK 4 FREE

Chapter 6 Price and Release Your Book

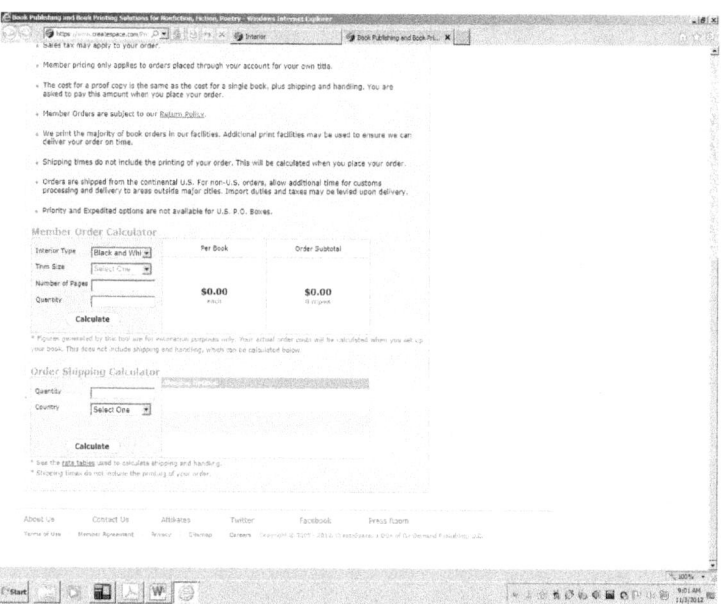

The page above pops up when you click on this link. Don't dwell too much on the pricing and costing of your product right now, you still have a lot of work to do.

The page above is accessible from the "Interior Page" where there is a link called "Estimate your manufacturing costs". If you enter the number of pages, the program will give you some idea of what your costs per book will be. I didn't take you there because it would have interrupted the flow. Now that you have completed the section, you could go back and play with the page, but why bother. The next page tells you the actual cost of your book and allows you to price it.

The following page is the important one when it comes to pricing because it's not only telling you your cost per book if you want to order hard copy, nut it allows you to tell Amazon what the retail price will be.

MAKE YOUR PAPERBACK 4 FREE

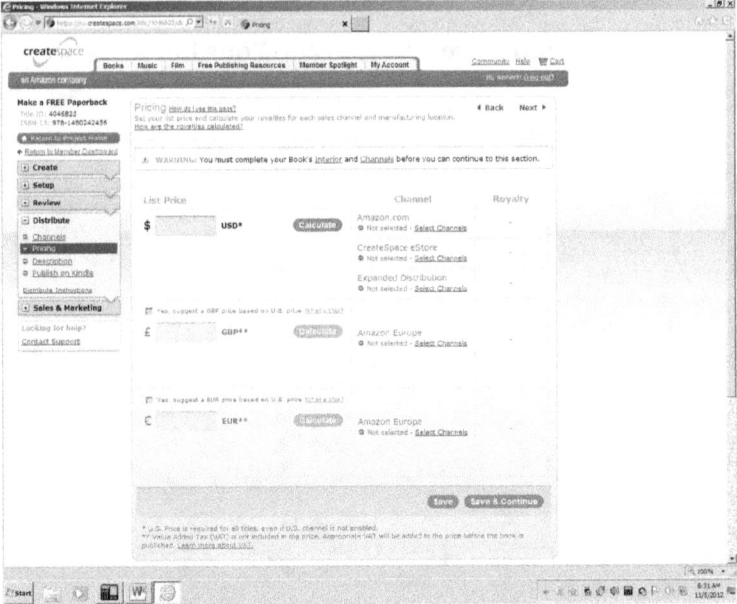

By setting the retail price, you control your "margine" which is your "royalty" commission.

The way I do this is to look at my cost, then add about 50% and check my royalty. I find that the thicker my book is, the smaller the percentage of my royalty. The cost of printing the book will effect the ceiling price that I'm comfortable charging.

Yet, with the higher priced thicker books, a lower percentage commission is still more money than the thinner lower cost books. It's a wash.

MAKE YOUR PAPERBACK 4 FREE

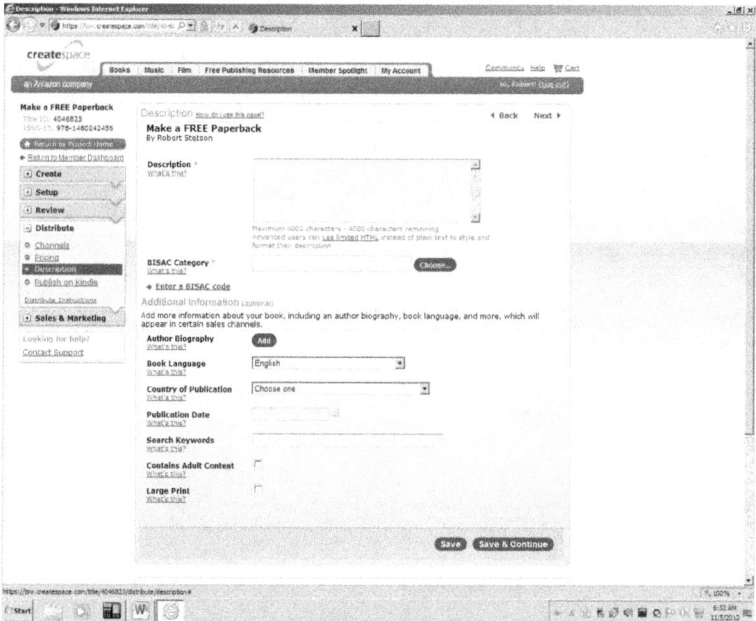

To sell your book, Amazon needs to tell prospective buyers what the book is about. Also, the prospective buyers who are doing searches while using key-words will find your book if you have the right information. If the buyer can't find your book, the buyer can't buy it.

The description of your book is very important because it is the only clue to what the book is about.

Unlike the EBooks, paperbacks don't have the ability to offer the first 10% of the book to the prospective reader. If the description isn't exciting to the buyer, they will move on to someone elses book. Paperbacks are more expensive than EBooks, so the customers are more discriminating.

Just as important as the description are the keywords. Keywords are used in the search process when people are looking for a book to read.

If a customer enters the keyword "adventure" but "adventure" is not among your keywords, then your book title will never be listed as a potential offering. You will have lost a sale before you ever got out of the gate, so think it through and choose your keywords carefully.

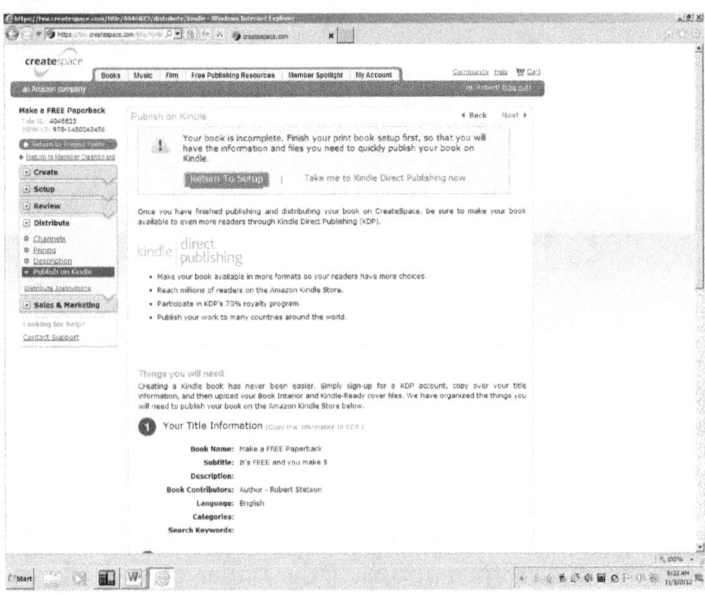

Direct publishing makes your book available to owners of Kindle, the EBook reader.

A word of caution here. The formatting requirements for an EBook are different than for a paperback, so don't just "whomp" your book interior over onto the EBook uploader. You will need to address the format differences.

If you go to Chapter 10, I will walk you through the major differences and help you get your book ready for the Kindle Store.

certified resellers such as independent bookstores and book resellers. The CreateSpace Direct program allows eligible resellers to buy books at wholesale prices directly from CreateSpace.

Select Sales Channels
Depending on your book's eligibility you can choose access to the Expanded Distribution channels by purchasing Expanded Distribution for $25. Then confirm your Standard Distribution and Expanded Distribution selection by clicking 'Save' or 'Save & Continue'.

Select Sales Channels
Depending on your book's eligibility you can choose access to the Expanded Distribution channels by purchasing Expanded Distribution for $25. Then confirm your Standard Distribution and Expanded Distribution selection by clicking 'Save' or 'Save & Continue'.

Set Your List Price
As the author, you set the list price for your book. You can change your book's list price at any time.

Enter Sales Information *
Create or edit your book's sales information, including description and an author biography. This information will be used in the sales channels you've chosen. You can change your book's list price at any time.

Chapter 7 Sit Back and Make the MONEY

If you want to make money, you have to have your books out there in the retail world, outside of the web.

Promote Your Book
Explore our Community, Resources, and Professional Services to get a jump start on your marketing strategy.

* Changes to your sales information can take 3-5 business days to appear on Amazon.com and 6-8 weeks to take effect through the Expanded Distribution Channel.

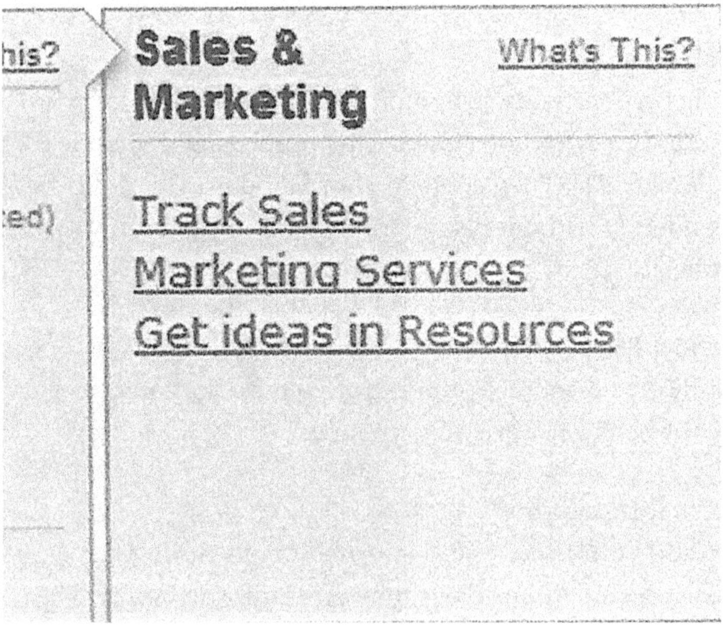

Sales & Marketing

What's This?

Track Sales
Marketing Services
Get ideas in Resources

Seems funny to say, but the bigger the boys, the less you have to do to get your items on the list of available products.

Strange to say, but if you "lend" a book, it's not like EBooks where you get it back. Kiss your book goodbye if you "lend" it to a friend. Either they won't give it back, "I lost it." Or they actually will lose it.

MAKE YOUR PAPERBACK 4 FREE

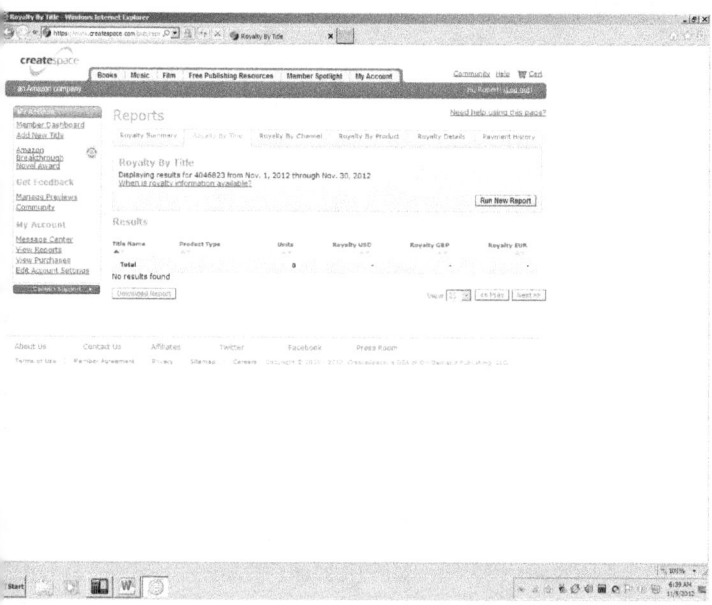

You have a royalty report by title available from Amazon right at your fingertips.

On the "Sales and Marketing" block, just click on "Track Sales" and you will have the "Reports" page for the book title you selected in the Dashboard. This is useful to keep tabs on the customer's traaffic activity for this specific toitle.

Use this tool to compare the sales for the various titles you own and determine which ones are selling best, or worse.

If you know which titles are not selling, you can work on determining the reason. The same goes for the best sellers. If Romance Novels all outsell Science Fiction you've written, you might want to focus on writing more Romance Novels, for example.

MAKE YOUR PAPERBACK 4 FREE

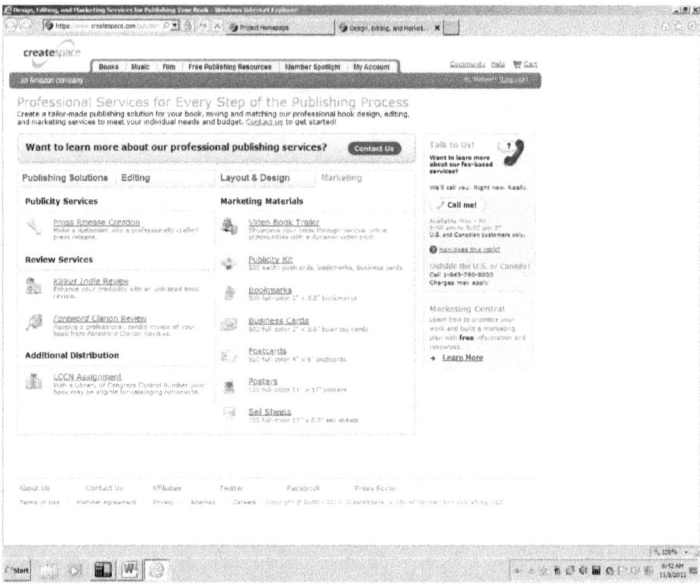

On the "Sales and Marketing" block, click on "Marketing Services" and you will have the "Professional Services for Every Step of the Publishing Process" page for the book title you selected in the Dashboard.

I won't create pages of dialog with regard to this page, because as you click on any item on the page, there are reams of information to guide you.

On the right side of the page is the most amazing feature I have ever seen.

Just click on the "CALL ME" button under the picture of a phone and you have the option to have them call you layer, or "CALL ME NOW".

The reponse is so quick you can't get your hand from the mouse to the phone before it rings.

61

MAKE YOUR PAPERBACK 4 FREE

Just as amazing is the fact that it's available 24 hours a day and 360 days a year. I do most of my work between 6:00 PM and 6:00 AM, so I really appreciate the quick and direct response.

The support staff is helpful and very friendly. They want to take the best care of their authors. After all, you are what pays the light bill over there. They haven't forgotten that.

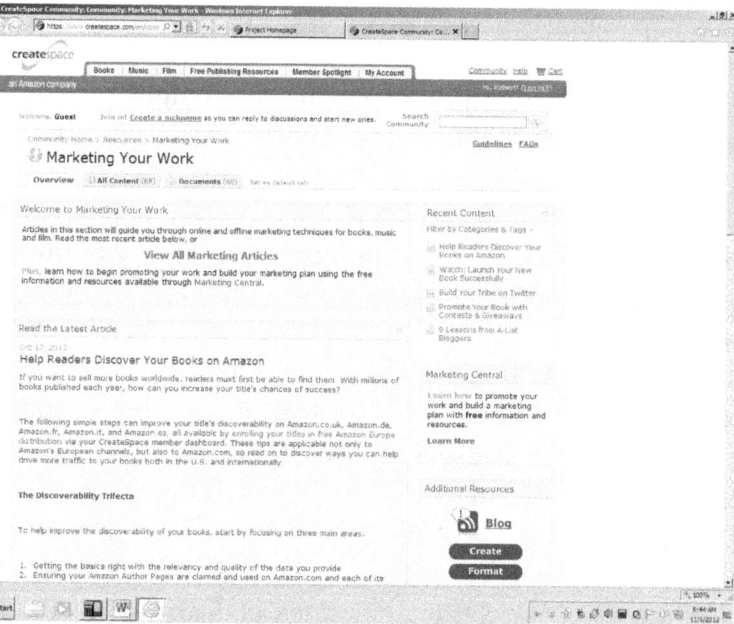

n the page "Marketing Your Work" there are plenty of articles and how to" information.

n the lower right hand corner you can see the "Blog Creator" where ou can Format and start your own Blog.

 don't have much time for blogging, but for those of you who are ocial butterflies, this is a great resource.

Chapter 9 Mistakes – I've Made a Few

Before getting involved in publishing I was a Computer Technologist for years and working as an Auxiliary Police Officer on patrol in the evenings. Then I was a Constable while working as a Real Estate Broker in the collapsing real estate market. I was a Licensed Private Detective for nine years total operating offices in two states.

The breadth and depth of my experience has taught me one thing, be gentle with your-self. Make your mistakes the kind you can fix.

I'm retired now and loving it. I'm busier than ever working night and day around the clock.

When it comes to writing, you will win a few and you will lose a few. There will be the book that nobody buys, and there will be the book that sells like hotcakes.

The message I want to leave you with is this. Don't give up. Writing is not an event, it's a process. We authors are a tough bunch of people. We suffer the slings and arrows of the critics and the reviewers who may not be as diplomatic as they could be.

No matter how crudely the review, bear in mind that you can learn from it. Something badly said is still something said. It's not personal.

A writer is much like a Venture Capitalist… All you need is ONE winner to make you rich. Hang in there, my friend.

Chapter 10 How to format your EBook

If you're reading this then you haven't published your EBook yet. The EBook format is different than the paperback book format.

Use MS Word 2010 to create your EBook pages, or you can cut and paste the text from the template to the MS Word document. When you have completed the transfer of all your pages, you will still not have an "EBook Ready document.

The lead in pages should not have the ISBN numbers. EBooks don't need ISBN Numbers, but even if you have already published a paperback, I would not include it. First off, the ISBN for the paperback is assigned by Amazon and is not the same. Second, you can point the reader to your paperback product by another means, which might result in another sale.

Don't forget to always put the copyright notice up front. As I've said before, it's the traditional place for it. If they don't see the copyright notice, they (they being the readers) will assume you don't have any property rights with regard to the document contents. This is especially true if they are just reviewing the first ten pages.

Now you're almost ready to upload the word document into the upload page, but not quite.

EBooks don't have headers, footers or page numbers so if you're converting a paperback document to EBook format you will have to remove these.

One of the things that make EBooks easier is that they don't require pagination. One of the most common mistakes new authors make is that by the time they finish tweaking the book content, they forget to recreate the Table of Contents.

Make sure when you create the table of contents that you go to the "References" tab in MS Word and click on "Table of Contents". If you've never made a table of contents before, you have to go to the bottom of the menu that drops down and click on "Insert table of contents".

An EBook table of contents is different than the paperback table of contents. In the EBook table of contents you have to uncheck the "Show Page Numbers" and check the "Use Hyperlinks instead of page numbers" options. This will allow the reader to select the paragraph by using the menu.

When you deselect the Page Number option it will automatically ignore the "Right Justify" option.

When I do the Paperback option, I use the page numbers, right justifies along with the Hyperlink option. It makes the editing job easier by allowing you to move around in the document more quickly without having to scroll as much.

When you set up the Menu, make sure you select only the types of headers you will be using. The "Show Levels" automatically comes up with three levels. Unless you have sub-headers and/or sub-sub-headers, change the number of headers to "1".

Don't be concerned about the hyperlink usage. The hyperlink blue print along with the characteristic underline is not visible even though they are hyperlinks.

By the way... Did you right justify your text? A professional looking book has smoothly aligned left and right edges. The "ragged edge look" is considered highly amateurish. That goes for printed books and EBooks alike.

Let's talk about how the headers should look. Make sure you use the "Heading Formats" located on the right hand side of the tool bar under the "Home" Tab.

For Primary Headers use the "AaBbCc Heading 1" for the chapter titles.

While we're talking about the Style Formats, make sure that for all of the regular text "AaBbCc Normal" is selected. You can tell which Style is selected by the yellow ring around the option box. If your text has a Style equal to the header style, the text will appear in the menu when you create it. That is a pain.

I always put the ISBN 10 and the ISBN 13 numbers on the first page of my EBook if I have them; it's just the way I do things. I want people to know the EBook is not only copyrighted, but that the copyright is registered with the copyright office.

Chapter 11 Get Crackin'

What are you reading this for? Put this damned book down and start writing. People want to buy your EBooks and paperbacks, but they're not available...yet.

ABOUT THE AUTHOR

After spending years trying to get my book into print, looking at "vanity publishing houses" and frustrated by the high cost of launching a paperback in the physical world, I came upon Amazon.

I have been writing and publishing a few books. Working through the learning process on Amazon while getting grounded in the art of getting it done right. Now I want to help others accomplish what I have on Amazon.com.

People need a guide to take them by the hand and take them through the process of getting their manuscript posted and selling. Most people make the same mistakes and sometimes the right way to do something isn't obvious. Follow this guide and get published, not just on the Internet, but how to make a paperback that they can wrap their fist around.

Log onto my Web Site for a link to Amazon.Com special deals and for information on other books I have written;

http://WWW.RobStetson.Com

www.ingramcontent.com/pod-product-compliance
Lightning Source LLC
Chambersburg PA
CBHW061517180526
45171CB00001B/215